TABLE OF CONTENTS

I0397036

INTRODUCTION

The Teacher Gets Schooled

Ever since I was in high school, I wanted to be a teacher and a coach. I tutored students in Algebra and Geometry. I gave private saxophone lessons to middle-school students. I worked in an elementary school daycare during my summers for a number of years before finishing college. I wanted to teach because I felt like America needed more smart, ambitious people in the classroom to inspire the next generation of youth. My sentiment on this topic has not changed.

After earning my teaching degree in 2006, I taught math and band for a couple of years in a small town in Northern Michigan. I loved the work I was doing and things were really going great. It was a lot of hard work, with every hour of class having a completely different set of lessons, but I enjoyed the pace and the kids were absolutely terrific. After my second year, I started on my Masters degree, and I felt like my teaching career was really taking hold.

In early January of 2009, I was driving along the coast of Lake Huron on a very cold, gray day on my way to work, when I noticed that I was driving by an incredibly long line, perhaps a half-mile, of people standing on the sidewalk all bundled up. I later learned that the line of people I saw was because the restaurant had one part-time server position open up, which over 700 people applied for that day. When I heard this, I shook my head and thought to myself "Thank God that isn't me. I'm a good teacher, I work really hard, and I'm glad my job is safe."

Three weeks later, I was approached by my school's administrators and was asked to not attend the state music conference which was scheduled on our teacher in-service day. Instead, I was asked to come in to meet with my building principal. When I came in the next morning, I was asked to immediately pack my classrooms up, because today would be my last day. I never got to say goodbye to my students, some of whom I had worked with for years.

Losing a job that I loved was an absolutely surreal feeling. I had never considered the idea of losing my job. I worked hard and received promotions in the organizations I volunteered for and the jobs I held. I had terrific grades throughout school, I earned scholarships, awards - yet none of this mattered. I felt empty, hollow, cold, confused, and had no idea what I would do next.

The Teacher Learns a Hard Lesson

A new reality emerged - I had about $4,000 in my bank account, over $40,000 in various loans, and no income. I was living in the county with the highest unemployment rate (25.7%, I looked it up that day) in the state with the highest unemployment rate in the country. It was like being punched so hard in the stomach that the wind was knocked out of my lungs. My pride was gone. The joy and excitement that used to light up my face and my mood were replaced with a somber dullness, the result of a sobering reality. I was more than broke - I was in deep debt and without a means to pay. It was at that point that I wondered, "If I am so smart, how in the world did I let myself get in this mess? Why didn't I plan better?"

There was no time to lick my wounds. I negotiated out of the lease on the house I was renting and immediately moved to Flint, Michigan. Yes, the Flint with lead water contamination and burnt-out factories and a violent crime rate higher than Baghdad. That Flint. It had substitute teaching jobs. As a substitute teacher, every morning I woke up at 5:00am to wait for a phone call. When I got the phone call for what school I would teach at, and which classroom I would be at for the day. After substitute teaching I would then drive to Lansing, 35 miles away, and tutor students until 8:30pm, drive back home, eat dinner, and go to bed. Five days a week, plus tutoring on Saturdays, and working retail on the weekends is how I lived.

For me, it was really depressing to be a substitute teacher. I was thankful to have work of course, but every day I had to step into another teacher's classroom, with another teacher's students. I had to watch their kids completing some half-baked form of busy work. When I taught, my classrooms had lots of posters and shapes, artwork that made you think, books for kids to read about all sorts of subjects and ideas, and hands-on activities for kids who needed something to squish or click to pay attention better. These classrooms were typically lifeless cinder-block rooms, sterile, and as empty as my heart felt. I clocked in, I proctored, stayed to the script, and clocked out. My heart broke.

As the months went by, I had a lot of time to think about where I had been and why I was doing what I was doing. I looked into job retraining programs, but when the state social worker asked me to take classes in how to use a word processor, my pride took over. I had some choice words for the social worker(which I later wrote an apology letter for) but that experience inspired me to find a way, any way, to get out of this financial hell of debt I made for myself.

Thankfully, a few months later I was able to earn a full-time job as an educational administrator, overseeing the business operations and management of a professional learning center in Jackson, Michigan. Now out of survival mode, I decided that it was time to really take a look at working and living differently. I was determined to never be in that type of financial straits ever again. I never, ever wanted to feel that lonely, that desperate, or that worthless again. I knew that meant not just spending less money, but actually learning about budgeting, about finances, about wealth and building for my future.

I rented a small one-bedroom apartment in the sub-floor of a building for $400/month. The bedroom and living room periodically flooded with water, and for the first couple of weeks my cats managed to catch an entire family of mice. I would come home, open the door, and be greeted with a tribute of a dead mouse at the entry. There was also the occasional cockroach or a centipede that inhabited the apartment with us. I had a DSL connection, but no cable. I didn't allow myself many luxuries; I rarely went out to eat, and only if I stayed late at work. For the next two and a half years, I worked my full-time job during the week then worked retail during the weekends, and paid back every last dollar I owed. I owed thousands of dollars on credit cards, medical bills, loans taken during college, and my car.

In 2012, seven years after graduating college and three years after losing my teaching job, I could finally say I was debt-free.

I am Now Worth Zero Dollars.

With no debt left to pay, I splurged. I ate out most nights, bought some new clothes, and started contemplating a new car. It was when I went out car shopping late one night that I stopped myself short, and asked myself one question.

"Steven, do you really want to go back there?"

In my head, a resounding "NO!" boomed. But another question came to mind.

"Why have I been spending again? Why is it so tempting?"

I pondered that question for a couple of days. I found myself wondering, "What would I do with my money if I didn't spend it? What COULD I do with my money if I didn't spend it, or what if I spent it differently?"

How did I want my future to look? I thought about the house I wanted to have for my future family. I wanted to raise kids and have parties for the entire community. I thought about traveling all over the world, seeing incredible and different places and meeting people from all walks of life. I thought about making sure my children didn't have to worry about loans for college, about driving a fast and sexy sports car, and about starting a non-profit and teaching for free when I retire.

That's when I decided that I needed to make smarter spending habits.

CHAPTER 1

Let's Make a Promise to Each Other

I am guessing that you didn't pick up this book to just keep doing the same thing, over, and over again. I am going to hypothesize that you want to take meaningful steps to change how you live, to rewire your thinking about your lifestyle, so you can have the lifestyle you actually want later on. I am guessing that sounds way more appetizing than a Big Mac or another caramel macchiato. But the bottom line is that it takes three key values that you need to possess in order for what I am going to show you to actually work.

1. Honesty
You know and admit, fully and completely, your faults. You will not hide from the truth of your actions; moreover, you will fully express your faults and shine a light on them,

2. Humility
You know what you have done in the past is wrong and it has not worked. You are flawed, and far from perfect in how you live your life. You have to work to do to become more self-aware, and you understand that it is a process and that it takes time.

3. Determination

You acknowledge that this new path you are heading down will be bumpy and that you will make mistakes along the way. You are committed to living a better life today so you can live an even better life tomorrow. To that end, you will do your best to completely execute what this book coaches you to do, thoughtfully considering what you are doing and why. You will create a better life for yourself because you do not consider any other reality acceptable.

This book is going to teach you over 28 days how to spend smarter. You are going to take concrete steps to improve how you spend your money, but you are also going to learn how to think differently about what you earn. We are going to dig deep into what you value, what you want to do with your life. Because we need to work from there to build better spending habits that reflect who you really are. These new habits will translate into changes in your day to day life, supported by what you value and how you think about your money.

I am a grown child who enjoys craft soda, Pac-Man and saving money every month by spending smarter.

CHAPTER 2

Low Battery

One of the most annoying things to my day is when I look down at my phone and see that it has a low battery. The reminders are annoying and they usually happen when it is the most inconvenient. I don't really think about it much when I am sitting at home, and most nights I forget to plug it in too. I might remember to plug my phone in during the morning when I brew my coffee, but that's usually for about 45 minutes while I get ready for the day, and then I unplug it with maybe a 50% charge and I hope for the best.

But some days . . . okay many days, my phone usage is fairly high. Emails and texts flow in. I get a call or two from friends, a call from Mom, and of course I have to share with my friends what I watched on YouTube the night before. By noon, I get that annoying message "20% battery remaining" and all I think is "oh not again!" So then I try to be more conservative, more judicious about my battery usage for about an hour, and then I forget and go right back to my social media sharing ways, until about 1:30pm when a notification pops up saying "10% battery remaining."

10% remaining? I can't believe how bad these phone batteries are. I then will grumble and rant while putting my phone DEEP into my pocket, hoping not to touch it again because later I am going shopping and I need my phone to compare prices and read reviews. I can hear my phone dinging with texts and emails, so I now ONLY check the emails and texts, hoping that my battery will hold up.

I finish the workday and get to the first store for some shopping, and as I look down at my phone, I notice that it is at 2%. I frantically start searching for the items I am shopping for, and just as the page is about to load up with everything I want and need to know...

It dies.

The phone shuts off. I keep pressing the power button, holding it, hoping it has made a mistake and will grant my request. But it doesn't.

Let's break down what happened.

I didn't plan to save the power I needed, because I didn't think about how much power I actually needed to live happily throughout the day. When I spent way too much, I tried to cut back, but my habits overcame my logical thinking and I went back to making bad actions. When I got really low on power, I cut my activities to what I considered "essentials," and yet even doing that, in the final hour, wasn't good enough.

This is what happens to millions of Americans every single year when it comes to managing their money. When it comes to our financial future, you would think that our decision-making would change because the stakes are higher, but they don't. Our spending translates into a lack of "power" in our bank account, keeping us from being able to do the things we want to do with our lives. At some point we may even become aware of the problem, and even try to change our behaviors, but we tend to fall back on our self-destructive spending habits because our philosophy, our understanding of how to better use our resources, hasn't changed.

These next 28 days are about transforming you by changing what you tend to do. Instead of leaving with half a battery and constantly draining it to zero, you need to build a full charge so that no matter what life throws at you, you are prepared to handle it. Building the foundation needed to live without fear takes time, and the idea of not living paycheck to paycheck may feel entirely foreign to you. Yet it is only when you stop living paycheck to paycheck that you can start building real wealth and having your work move you step-by-step toward your long-term life and financial goals.

Are You a Typical American?

No one thinks of themselves as "typical." How different is the "typical American life" or the "average" American life to yours? The way you live and the things you struggle with on a day to day basis are things that only you battle through. It can feel like you are trying to run on a financial tightrope, hoping that no one cuts the line out from behind you. It can be lonely, it certainly can be frustrating, and even when things feel like they might improve, Murphy's Law rears its head in and suddenly you get sick, or you blow a tire on your car, and you are right back where you started . . . or worse. It can be easy to wonder if there is something wrong with you.

Are you a bad person? Not at all. But you know and I know that what is happening in your financial life may not be the best way to live. Over the next 28 days, this is exactly what we are going to work on together

I think a good place to start when thinking about our finances is to open up about what other people experience with their finances. It helps put your unique situation into perspective. Here are a few key facts about Americans and our financial lives from a recent Fed Survey of Household Economics and Decision Making.

1. About 46% of adults say they cannot cover an emergency expense of $400 without selling something or borrowing money. Now consider, 18% of those surveyed said that either they or family members living with them have had some financial hardship in the last year such as a health emergency, employment problems, or a divorce.
2. Despite the availability of health care coverage, 20% of people report that they don't get dental care and 12% go without seeing a doctor due to health-care costs.
3. 31% of non-retired adults have no retirement savings or pension at all, including about half of respondents ages 18-29. Only 22% of Americans age 60 and older have $100,000 or more saved for retirement.

So guess what? YOU ARE NOT ALONE! Not even close! Many people struggle in the same ways you struggle, but there is one key difference between you and them: You are taking steps to spend smarter.

Just by reading this book, you are different. You want something different and better for yourself, and you are going to take the steps towards making changes. This journey is going to challenge your thinking and what you do. At times, it might feel like it challenges how you live your life. I won't apologize - it will challenge how you live, because the goal is not to "do the same thing and hope for a different result." You need to spend smarter to pursue a different result, because at the end of this I want you to live more sustainably and improve your personal finances.

Are you hungry for change? Are you starving for a new way to look at how you treat the money you earn? Are you salivating at the idea of a healthier bank account? Let's go!

Eating Into Your Earnings

When I work with new clients, we begin by talking about their personal budget. They are usually very proud of how low their rent is, their cable bill, their utilities, and that they have already cut something out of their budget. Some cut manicures and pedicures, while others watch streaming videos instead of going to the movies, or going shopping only when they really need a new piece of clothing instead of going every week. The kicker is, for an average middle-class household, entertainment and apparel account for less than 10% of their total spending. But at the end of the conversation, I ask one of the most important questions, "How much do you spend on food?"

And then their eyes shift down, or to the side, as though they didn't hear me. So I ask again, leaning in, "what do you spend on food each month?" The answer I usually get, accompanied by a nervous laugh, is usually "A lot" or "Way more than I should." So then I ask again "Now, how do you spend on food each month?" And almost everyone's response is "I eat out way too much."

Do you eat out too much? Be honest, because it is the only way to actually identify a problem and act on it. Are you getting a latte every morning, and going out to lunch three or four days a week, and then grabbing an easy fast food meal on your way home most days of the week?

It is okay to feel frustrated as you look as these questions and think "geez, that's me." I'll be open with you - that was me too. I used to get coffee out every day of the week, and have food ordered in every day at work, AND go out for dinner most nights or get a pizza on my way home. When I was out on the road for work, it was easy to pull into the local fast-food restaurant and get items from their Dollar Menu. But you better believe I paid for it - I ballooned in weight, I didn't feel good after eating all that junk, and you better believe I was sinking a fortune into it, all because I had no good way to handle the stress of the day. And that's me as a never married, no kids twenty-something-year old guy. For you, things might look a little different. You have stress, kids, a partner, demanding jobs and more responsibilities than I can imagine.

Knowing your life, and your reality, doesn't change the end result. How we eat can be destructive to our bank accounts. You probably have heard the phrase "the ends does not justify the means" and this is no exception. Lots of people have lots of problems, but it doesn't give you ground to stand on, trading a small amount of personal edification today for more problems with your finances and your health later on down the road.

The first thing we need to do is to understand how you perceive your spending. Most of my clients perceive that they spend far less than they actually do. I will take an educated guess that you may be the same way. Yet, how you perceive your spending to be plays a major role in the other financial decisions you make.

How much money do you think you spend a month on food? When you purchase food, where are you buying it from? Be specific, but don't cheat and look at your credit card account yet!

Monthly food expenses: _____

Food expenses description:

_____

_____

_____

_____

_____

Over the next several days, you will be drilling down into your food spending habits. Often times, what we think we do and what we actually do are different. We are going to explore just how wide that gap is, what causes you to make decisions that don't align with your goals, and how to change your mindset about those decisions so that you make better ones. When you make better individual decisions, you will start to build healthy spending habits, which is the key in building the financial stability and future you are looking for.

DAY 2

Habitually Eating Your Earnings

Most people believe they have a strong understanding of their behaviors. Some families I work with even have spreadsheets showing me each dollar they budget every month, and it looks great - in the spreadsheet. Yet when I dig into their bank account statements, about 95% of the time I find substantial inconsistencies between their spreadsheet world and the reality. Most people get anxious when they think about money, so they avoid the subject altogether, which can create a spending "blind spot." It's time to move away from financial denial, for you to own how you are spending your money and to make different choices so you spend less.

Yesterday, I asked you to write down what you "thought" you were doing, but to not look it all up. I now want you to pull up statements from your recent credit card bills and bank accounts. I want to focus only on food transactions and answer the following survey questions honestly.

1. How often do you go to the grocery store?
   a. Three times a week or more.
   b. Twice a week.
   c. Once a week.
   d. Once every other week or less.

2. How much do you spend each month on groceries? _____

3. How often do you go to specialty coffee shops or convenience stores?
   a. Four times a week or more.
   b. 2-3 times a week.
   c. Once a week.
   d. Less than once a week.

4. How much do you spend each month on coffee/convenience dining? _____

5. How often do you eat out for lunch?
   a. Four times a week or more.
   b. 2-3 times a week.
   c. Once a week.
   d. Less than once a week.

6. How much do you spend each on month on eating out for lunch? _____

7. How often do you eat out for dinner/date night/drinks?

    a. Four times a week or more.

    b. 2-3 times a week.

    c. Once a week.

    d. Less than once a week.

8. How much do you spend each month on dinner/date night/drinks?

_____

Total up #2, 4, 6, and 8. _____

Feel beat up? That's an okay thing to feel after doing this. But let's put this into perspective: According to recent surveys conducted by CNN Money, Americans on average spend $5,200 a year on food. That is literally $100 a week just on food! No one NEEDS to spend $100 a week to eat in this country. Even if you need almond milk and gluten-free everything, I am sincerely confident that you can do that on less than $100 a week. We will be working together to improve these habits and this spending over the next several days.

DAY 3

Eating Smarter to Spend Smarter

S o, you might be asking yourself why I asked you to answer all those questions about how often you eat at various places and times. I believe that simply telling you to "spend less on food" doesn't actually tell you HOW to spend less on food. It defines a desired outcome, but without changing your behaviors, habits and lifestyle, it is unlikely that you will change the outcome. People have this false notion that "if I only had a budget, then I would save more money!" Spreadsheets and budgets alone do not help you save more money because spreadsheets and budgets do not change the decisions you make when you choose to spend money - your habits do. You have to be willing to change your habits to spend smarter to earn a better outcome.

Over the next few days, you will be creating a brand new food spending schedule. For each of the survey questions on Day 2, especially where you answered A or B, I would like you to move down one answer with your habit change for this first month. For example, if you typically go to the grocery store five days a week, I would like you to try scheduling and sticking with two grocery shopping trips a week. Adjust your habits, but avoid the temptation of making a big change too quickly. Making too big of a change too rapidly typically results in a relapse to the old habit, so be patient. Be purposeful when you go grocery shopping, what day(s) you get a coffee treat, or go out for lunch, or go on date night/out on the town. Remember, we create new habits by changing old behaviors, and right now that requires a deliberate act on your part. Be specific and stick to it!

Let's start with grocery shopping. If you are going to the grocery store every other day, you are typically buying fresh food you intend to eat that day or the next day, but may be prone to overspending because the tendency will be to purchase whatever you are craving that day. By reducing the number of trips, it will require more planning of what is being bought, but it also gives you the opportunity to take advantage of deeper discounts on items, to stockpile foods you like, and to avoid impulse purchases that may either lead to overeating or losing food to spoilage. I also recommend purchasing meat and other expensive perishable foods in bulk, breaking them down, and freezing the portion you don't need for later - this often saves me 30-50% off regular market price. Typically, I personally aim for $150/month (about $35 per week) as my budget for groceries, and I shop for groceries on Mondays.

How often/what days will you go grocery shopping now?

_____

Multiply the last number by 4.3
(This is your new monthly convenience budget.) _____

How much money did you save?

_____ - _____ = _____
Old Budget   *New Budget*   *Total Savings*

As you begin transitioning from spending on services to spending on groceries, a concern that frequently comes up is whether you will go over your budget on the groceries. Focus less on the cost of the groceries to begin with, and put more energy in making sure you shop for groceries on a consistent basis. Trust me, just the act of trading back fast food and convenience dining for groceries and making meals at home will save you money. You will eventually become a skilled shopper and your grocery bills will go down to reflect it.

Is Starbucks Sipping Away Your Savings?

I love specialty coffee with a fierce passion. My license plate frame even says, "Outta my way, I'm going to Starbucks!" I used to go get coffee pretty much every day, which cost me after tip about $5.00 a day, and then I would buy some coffee for home too. I didn't think much of it until I looked at my spending while doing my taxes, only to find that I spent over $1,600 that year on Starbucks. That is a mountain of beans if I ever saw one! Now, when I go, I typically purchase whole-bean coffee to brew at home, and only go once a week as a treat (typically Tuesdays) to myself or to meet a client (which is also a treat for me).

Many people who go out go purely out of convenience. By convenience I mean coffee shops, gas stations, places you pick up a snack and/or a beverage. Consider this: For each day you reduce your "morning fix," you may save yourself $260 and 20,800 calories A YEAR. That is like losing nearly 6 pounds. Take this a step further: if you can cut down four days a week to two, or three days a week to one, that's $520, 12 pounds. Now let's say each visit takes ten minutes - you just saved 17 hours of your life, nearly a full day per year waiting in line for a beverage. Do this for thirty years, and you gain three weeks of your life back, 360 pounds, and $15,600.

To help get you started, here are some of my favorite tips to help you keep this new habit of making breakfast in the morning.

1. **Set a reminder to eat breakfast at home:** Make sure to put in your calendar, on your phone a reminder, or even a sticky note on your refrigerator, or even a sticky note on the inside of your front door, to eat breakfast at home.
2. **Plan ahead:** Set your alarm clock earlier back so you actually have time to make the coffee and eat.
3. **Grab and go:** Prepare a few breakfast sandwiches or a snack that you can quickly grab if you don't get up on time. You can even store these in the freezer in reusable bags or containers and reheat them at the office.

How often/what days will you go convenience dining now?

_____

_____

How much will you spend a week?   _____

Multiply the last number by 4.3

(This is your new monthly convenience budget.)   _____

How much money did you save?

_____ - _____ = _____

Old Budget   *New Budget*   *Total Savings*

Remember that spending smarter is not just about spending less. Spending smarter is also about living smarter, with different habits and planning ahead. You need to be prepared so that even when you wake up late, or the car won't start, or the pet gets sick on the carpet, you have a way of handling that situation without it ripping apart your wallet.

Don't let your spending whip you.

Make Lunch Boxes Great Again!

Work is stressful. Today, many benefits packages are substantially worse than they were in the 1990's and early 2000's, and with the cost of housing, healthcare, and education rising rapidly, we have to work longer and harder to get to the same point. Combine this with needing additional schooling, kids, and the pressures of everyday life, and it's no wonder that we eat out more often. It seems like eating out takes a pressure off of us - it helps us avoid one additional task, one more thing to think about during the day.

The problem is, this trade-off has a huge cost. Eating out can cost 60 to 100% more than purchasing the same groceries to prepare at home, and even more once you factor in tip, beverages, and transportation. If you typically spend $10 on lunch, each day of the week you pack your lunch saves you $520 a year. If you can knock out two days where you pack instead of eating out, that's $1,040 a year. Figure out what day(s) you plan to eat out, and on the other days . . . pack your lunch!

How often/what days will you go out for lunch now?

_____

How much will you spend a week? _____

Multiply the last number by 4.3
(This is your new monthly convenience budget.) _____

How much money did you save?

_____ - _____ = _____

Old Budget   _New Budget_   _Total Savings_

Now that you see the savings involved in packing a lunch, let's plan when you are going to prepare your lunch. Do you have enough time during the morning to pack a lunch then, or do you need to pack it the day before? If you are cooking meals with leftovers, can you pack the leftovers into smaller containers to easily grab on your way out the door? Do you want to pack each a lunch each day, or can you pack several days worth of lunches at the same time? In the space below, write down how you are going to pack lunches so that you avoid ordering in.

_____

_____

_____

_____

Date Night Does Not Mean Debt Night

D ate night is a great thing to have in your life. Going out with the girls, beer with the bros, or wine and dine and networking events are all good social activities to have in your life. If you have kids, between picking them up from school or daycare, taking them to their extracurricular and family activities, and making sure they do their homework, the last thing you may think about or feel like you have energy for is cooking dinner. Taking some pressure off by hitting the drive-thru, having food delivered, or hitting the local pub to pour a few down after a long day may sound like the best idea in the heat of the moment.

The kicker is, everyone's budget is different, and most people cannot afford and should not go out several times a week. Keep in mind the statistics of what a "typical American" looks like. Many of your friends may share the same worries about paying the bill at the end of the night or may be going through a financial or life hardship of their own. You have the opportunity to take the lead for the group in making a more thrifty activity choices and take the pressure off of your silent, but incredibly thankful friends.

With that in heart, let's take a look at your "going out" habits.

$ 28

How often/what days will you go out for dinner now?

_____

How much will you spend a week? _____

Multiply the last number by 4.3
(This is your new monthly convenience budget.) _____

How much money did you save?

_____ - _____ = _____
Old Budget _New Budget_ _Total Savings_

Find other activities to fill your social calendar, such as joining a running club, a book club, or volunteer at a non-profit organization. Consider hanging out with your friends at home, and take turns hosting. Look on social media platforms for free and low-cost activities in your area. Wherever your passions lie, plan your date/social nights and enjoy them, but a little careful planning can go a long way to you having more green in your bank account at the end of the month.

Make It Happen!

Now that we have broken down your food spending AND the habits that caused the food spending, I have one final task for you on this topic. Let's see just how much money you could save this month, just on trimming the food budget. Look back at your final totals for each of the days listed and write that final number in the space provided.

I am saving $_____ a month on groceries. (Day 3)

I am saving $_____ a month on convenience dining. (Day 4)

I am saving $_____ a month on lunch dining. (Day 5)

I am saving $_____ a month on going out for dinner. (Day 6)

Take the four numbers of how much you save in each area, add them up, and write that number here: $_____

Think about that number for a minute, and think about the process you just went through. This number is your grocery and dining target, your goal for the next month, to meet or exceed spending that much less. It will take some time to build these habits, but if you adopt them as a new way of living day-to-day, what you are going to find is that you are probably just as happy, if not happier with your life, even though you're having to make more food and do more of these things for yourself. You might also enjoy going out or grabbing that coffee a bit more, because it becomes a treat for you to have instead of "just another day in the coffeehouse."

Getting Your Hands-On Your Money!

One of the challenging aspects of bank accounts and credit and debit cards is that we cannot physically see the money we spend. We don't physically hand money over when we pay for most of the things we buy everyday and as a result it's easy to lose track of our spending. Mobile apps and online shopping actually make this problem worse, because you don't even have to pull out a card. On many applications, you can make a purchase with just a couple taps or a swipe of the phone, and at many stores just holding your mobile device up to the payment terminal is all it takes to buy something.

One way of adding a physical barrier and improving your resistance to impulse purchases is to use physical cash instead of your cards to pay for items. By using cash, you are now being forced to see your money leave your wallet every time you buy something - from a psychological standpoint, it is harder to physically surrender something you hold, so this practice creates a level of resistance. It also builds awareness, because you will see and feel every dollar you spend leave you.

Some people feel more comfortable than others with this method. Having significant amounts of cash physically on you may make you feel insecure, and that's okay. If that's the case, consider a habit of withdrawing enough cash to pay for your food budget, while keeping recurring payments like utilities and housing as an automatic, recurring payment. If you become more comfortable, include withdrawing a weekly amount that also includes other categories of your spending, and keep them in separate wallets. This will help you make sure that you stay on budget by only spending what you have in your wallet for that item - the grocery wallet pays for groceries, the pet wallet pays for pet supplies, etc. Take only the wallet for the things you are shopping for, and don't borrow from other wallets. Instead, change how you spend to stay on budget.

I know you can do this - I believe that your strength and desire to improve your situation is greater than the temptation. I want you to have a better life, and I know you want you to have a better life.

Congratulations on making it through the first seven days!
Use the calendar below to plan your weekly treats, groceries and other food habits.

My Weekly Plan
Monday
Tuesday
Wednesday
Thursday
Friday

Think About Why

Hopefully you have set a new budget for food, scheduling when your "treat" opportunities are and saving money by sticking to that new plan. As we keep working together, my hope is that you are not only saving more money each month, but by taking some financial pressure off you are then able to devote energy toward relieving some of the other pressures and stresses in your life. That is what I want to focus on today. Think about your life, the bigger picture, and what you want from it. What is holding you back?

Are you starting to realize that the choices you were making before weren't rational? You are absolutely correct! Our decisions many times are not rational at all. How you feel absolutely contributes in governing what you do. When how you feel dominates your thoughts, you lose awareness of aspects of your spending like how much you actually spend and what the long-term effect of it is. It might feel great scoring that new pair of shoes for the deal you got, but did you need them? In many cases, what you are doing to cope with the stress, and the resources it takes to do those things may actually be a culprit for WHY you are stressed and WHY you can't seem to get ahead. This process is about rooting out the financial culprits holding you back so you break the bonds of bad spending, oppressive debt, and anything else standing between you and the things dearest and most important to you.

Over the next few days, you will be writing about your life. Some of will be about financial things, but some questions will be just about you, who you are, and what it's like to walk in your shoes. Financial challenges and personal challenges affect virtually everyone at some point in their life. Many times, what is happening in your financial life, including the chaos that can happen, is really a reflection of your behaviors, which mirror how you feel. By identifying and better understanding what is happening in your life and how it is affecting you, you can become more aware of what you do to cope in those situations. That awareness is the key to changing your behavior (spending in a certain way) which then helps put you back in control.

What is Important to You - Survey

This next exercise spans a period of three days. Take time today to clearly write an answer to each of these prompts. The next day, come back to it and re-read the prompts, what you wrote, and then write some more.

Question 1:
List the 5 most important things in your life.

Day 8

1. _____

2. _____

3. _____

4. _____

5. _____

Day 9

1. _____

2. _____

3. _____

4. _____

5. _____

Day 10

1. _____

2. _____

3. _____

4. _____

5. _____

Question 2:

If you were to take that list, and now reduce it to three most important things, write those 3 things in order. After you do that, write for each one why it is one of the most important things in your life and what you want to do to improve it or enjoy it more.

Day 8

1. _____

_____

2. _____

_____

3. _____

_____

Day 9

1. _____

_____

2. _____

_____

3. _____

_____

Day 10

1. _____

_____

2. _____

_____

3. _____

_____

What is Stressful to You?

Today, we are going to break down a major reason why people slip into old habits and compensate with spending - stress. When you are stressed, you have a natural tendency to try and do things that will help make your life easier in the short-term, even if there are long-term consequences for it. By identifying what stresses you, you will become more aware of the situations that can trigger you to spend money needlessly. When you are in these situations in the future, you will have a greater ability to allow your logic to catch up with your emotions, which in turn means you making a healthier spending choice.

List the 5 most stressful things in your life.

1. _____

2. _____

3. _____

4. _____

5. _____

If you were to take that list, and now reduce it to three most stressful things, write those 3 things in order.

1. _____

2. _____

3. _____

What are the two things you spend the most on to cope with your stress or make your life less stressful? Is it coffee in the morning or beer and wine in the evening? Weekly massage or spa treatment? Write it down!

1. _____

2. _____

Take the three most important things in your life from Day 10 and the two things you spend the most on to cope with your stress from Day 11. Rank them in order from #1-#5, where #1 is the most important and #5 is the least important.

1. _____

2. _____

3. _____

4. _____

5. _____

The next couple of days, read aloud at the start of the day, in front of a mirror, what is most important to you. Start that statement with "The three things that are most important to me are _____."

You could even take a dry erase marker or sticky notes and write them on your mirror as a reminder. At the end of the day, right before you go to bed, do the same thing. Every day, what happens in between and the decisions you make will either contribute to those three things, or will detract from those three things. Why am I asking you to do this? Because when you remember who and what you are fighting for, it can be much easier when you get to a decision point to make the right choice.

The Important Things Vs. The Coping Things

Today, we are going to put together all the thoughts and ideas about what you value and deem important, what you do to cope with stress and problems, and put those things into perspective.

Trading Back Convenience for Cost

We touched on this subject earlier in breaking down food costs, that you have been conditioned to pay for the service of food as much or more than you pay for the food itself. Your entire first week was essentially devoted to cutting back on the fast/casual dining. When you made the decision to cut back on the coffee runs, the fast food, and eating out to brew your own coffee and make your own meals, you made the decision to trade back those services for the money you spent on those services. This is trading back convenience for cost.

You may not realize this, but you pay through your taxes and charitable contributions for a number of services that you potentially duplicate in your spending behaviors. A very common one is purchasing books. Whether you are buying a digital book or a physical one, it has become very convenient, practically instantaneous, for you to purchase and have access to nearly any book in print. But did you know that most libraries facilitate electronic books as well, and that you may be able to check out eBooks onto your electronic device from the comfort of your home? Most people remember the library from their experiences as a child - the card catalogue, or computer databases that were slow, and waiting days if not weeks to check out a book that was highly sought after. But libraries have changed, just like our lifestyles have changed, and many have shifted their focus to be a hub of media, not just a place to read musty books and old magazines.

And let's be blunt - when you finish a book, how often do you need daily access to that book. Would you be okay downloading it again for free to read it again . . . for free? If you check out just one book a month instead of buying it, assuming an average eBook bestseller costs $6.94, you save $30 a month, or $360 a year, just by checking it out at the library instead of purchasing it from a large Internet retailer.

Here is a list of other services you may already be paying for. Are you using them?

Visit Your Local Parks and Recreation Centers instead of going to the movies. Going hiking, walking, camping, and taking your kids to play on the playground promotes an active lifestyle and it's fun, be it on a date or with the entire family. Local parks are typically free for residents, and state/national parks and nature centers may be free or a very low cost to visit depending on the state, including cost-saving annual passes. You can save even more money by packing a lunch to enjoy on your adventure. This beats the pants off of $10-$15 tickets and another $10 a person for terrible food that you never wanted to begin with.

Participate in Community Education Programs and Online Courses instead of paying for an expensive yoga class at the gym.

Libraries, churches, schools, and other organizations offer free opportunities for kids and adults to learn new skills and gain unique experiences working with local expert volunteers in the community. This is a great way to bond with new people, make new friendships, and network in a relaxed setting without ripping your budget to shreds.

Give Back through Volunteer Opportunities instead of going out to an expensive club. Every community has its needs, and you don't have to raise a ton of money for a fancy trip to give back your time and talents to help others in need. Become a math or reading tutor for an elementary school student, or help work at your local food bank or soup kitchen. For me, I stream video games online with donations benefiting Extra Life, a charity that partners with the Children's Miracle Network. Find a cause that speaks to you and volunteer - you will feel great helping others and it does not have to cost you money to help.

Visit the Local Museum or Art Gallery instead of traveling out of town for the weekend. Take in some beautiful artwork and let your mind wander for an afternoon. Many galleries and exhibits as part of receiving Federal funding offer free days or free weekends periodically for anyone to visit. Block out some time and go see artwork from around the world and avoid the expense of hotel, transportation, and eating out.

Write down at least two conveniences other than food that you are willing to trade-off to save the cost. Let's see just how many services are willing to swap convenience for cost - the savings may be eye-opening for you.

Convenience	Cost/Month	New Habit	Cost/Month

How much money did you save?

_____ - _____ = _____
Total Cost of Conveniences   *Total Cost of New Habits*   *Total Savings/Month*

Digging Deep

There are many things people do to cope with stress, from shopping and food to smoking and alcohol. Almost no one believes that smoking is more important than their kids, their home, or their spouse. Yet if you smoke a half a pack a day, you choose to spend $1,500 a year on something dangerous, while instead you could have used that money to help fund your child's college education, save for retirement, or any number of goals you have. The last week hammered on buying food and eating, which is another major coping behavior where we consume thousands of extra dollars in food cost annually. What are you missing, what are you giving up in your life or with your family because of your spending? Is it worth the trade?

Subscription Services Suck Savings!

Iwill be the first to confess that I subscribe to services. I'm an avid Amazon Prime subscriber and I get two news publications - the Economist and Investors' Business Daily. I pay a monthly fee for my finance software and my website. I also enjoy video games and the WWE network. According to my fiancée Amber, I am a grown child.

Subscription services are a tried-and-true sales mechanism that have found new life in the digital age. With regular, smaller transactions automatically withdrawn monthly or annually, it is much easier for companies to help consumers digest large, annual fees by breaking them up into smaller parts. People are hesitant to spend $200 a year on a piece of software all at once, but gaining access to that software for less than $20/month sounds much more reasonable to the customer. If this sounds like a sales tactic, it is! We'll talk more about sales tactics and how to conquer them later in this book.

Does this mean I am going to ask you to cut your favorite streaming service or periodical or wine of the month out of your life? Not exactly. But what I do question and what I want you to explore is how much you actually use the services you pay for - that is to say, how much value do you get from your monthly subscriptions.

During one of our first budgeting sit-downs, Amber and I listed out every subscription service we had, how much we paid, and how much use we got out of it. When we did this, we noticed some redundancies. For example, we watched Amazon Video about 3 hours a week, or about 14 hours a month, but only watched Netflix 4 hours a month - when a good movie was available. But Amazon Video also has a rental option, so by renting the two movies a month we were watching on Netflix instead and canceling the service, we saved about $5 a month, good for $60 saved a year.

I also saw that my iPad had a cellular package for $25 a month, but 95% of the places I use my iPad have WiFi, and those that don't I could just download a book or game or software to use in advance. Cutting that expense out saved us another $300 a year, so just those two changes put another $378 a year in our pocket.

List below the subscription services you use, how often you use them, and how much a month you pay for them. Then, take a look at the list and see what services you actually need, what you actually use, and what services you can cut back or cut out altogether. At the bottom of the list, write down the dollar amount that you are going to save from cutting those subscriptions back. Finally, contact those companies and trim your subscriptions. You do NOT actually save the money until you ACT by canceling the service.

Name of Service	How Often Used?	How much/month?
1.		
2.		
3.		
4.		
5.		
6.		
7.		
8.		
9.		
10.		

Total Amount Per Month I Will Save: _____

Conserve Energy and Save Green

Conservation can sometimes be a pain in the butt. When you are home, you might really enjoy the warmth of having all the lights on, or taking a relaxing bath at the end of a long day. Maybe you never have considered that scraping your dishes to remove food left over instead of using water, changing your light bulbs, or the temperature of water you use to clean your clothes could have a meaningful impact on your wallet. Thinking about how you live day-to-day and being deliberate about the mundane activities and chores around the home can actually save you some serious green!

Here is a checklist of five different ways you can optimize your energy usage just by taking some easy alternative steps, along with how much you could potentially save according to ENERGY STAR, the energy rating program. As you go through the list, give yourself monthly credit for each task you complete, and total how much money you may be saving at the bottom of the list.

1. Replace your light bulbs with ENERGY STAR qualified compact fluorescent light bulbs (CFL's). Replacing your five most frequently used light bulbs or fixtures can save you $60 a year or more in energy costs and last 6-10 times longer than incandescent bulbs, meaning you will also replace these bulbs less often. That's a big savings for a pretty easy activity!

_____ (+$5 a month if you did this)

2. Consumer electronics account for up to 15% of the total energy cost in your home. A device that is "off" but plugged in is still being supplied with power. Just by turning off computers, laptops, tablets, your TV, and unplugging devices when you are finished charging them, you could save up to $60 a year by actually removing power supplied to devices not in use. An easy way to do this is to use a power strip to provide power and to turn off the power strip after use.

_____ (+$5 a month if you did this)

3. Wash your laundry with cold water whenever possible. Heating water accounts for 90% of the energy used to wash your clothes, so switching your loads from hot and warm to cold water saves a ton of energy, to the tune of $214 per year. That's savings you can spin cycle about!

_____ (+$18 a month if you did this)

4. Scrape the food from your dishes instead of rinsing them. Every minute you leave your tap on, you waste up to 6 gallons of water a minute. Rinsing your dishes for even a couple of extra minutes practically doubles the amount of water used to actually clean your dishes. Trust your dishwasher - scrape your dishes and save some dough.

_____ (+$3 a month if you did this)

5. Install a programmable thermostat to adjust your home's temperature settings when you are asleep or away. Having a thermostat that optimizes this can save you $150 a year in energy costs, and many of them connect to WiFi so you can manage it even if you are on vacation.

(+$12 a month if you did this)

_____

Total Potential Monthly Savings:

_____

Energy usage is more than just about environmental conservation. Just like our food spending, our energy spending is about consumption and convenience. Recognize that many of the ideas in this section should, thanks to the power of smarter technology, actually make your life easier to manage and less stressful. Take advantage of these solutions so you spend smarter by living smarter.

Where Do You Want to Be When You Grow Up?

You live in a fast-paced and unpredictable world. Stresses and challenges can come from any aspect of your life, and at times it may feel like a never-ending tornado of activity. As you work to build a rock-solid financial foundation, it can be easy to get so caught up in the work involved to save money, that you lose sight of why you are doing what you are doing. The problem with that is that when you forget why you're doing something, you leave yourself vulnerable to temptation, because giving in to temptation is more attractive than the "nothing" you may feel you get in reaching your financial goals.

This is certainly true of physical fitness as well. Every year, many people make a New Year's resolution to get in better shape (32.4% of people in 2017). So they start going to the gym and they eat better . . . for about a week. As the weeks drag on, they begin to start compromising their behavior, because they start to forget what the goal is. Of course they want to get in better shape, because health is important. But they don't have an idea in their mind what they want their final shape, their physical form, to look like. So, it's easier when tempted with chicken wings and burgers to "compromise" just for a meal or two. Within a month, 41.6% have already quit their journey, and according to the University of Scranton, just 8% actually reach their goals.

I believe a major factor of why the 8% actually reach their goals is that they know what their goals are. They don't just say "I want to be in better shape" but they set goals like "I want to run a half-marathon in August" or "I want to bench press X pounds more each month." They set specific, measurable goals that they can achieve in a reasonable period of time. They work through a plan that, step by step, gets them from where they are at now to where they want to be, and then they execute that plan, and then they SUCCEED.

You have already made some tremendous strides in improving your spending, saving more money this month than you probably imagined before opening the cover of this book. You have started to figure out what is important in your life, and that how you cope with stress is not as important as what you actually value in your life. You are now going to drill this down even further by starting to figure out what your finish line looks like.

How do you think you might want to live as you get older? What sort of house or apartment do you want to live in? Any particular vehicle you want to drive, or clothes you want to wear, or a part of the country you want to be in? Small town, big city, in the mountains, or on a beach?

What do you want to do? What level of lifestyle you want? What types of things might you want to do? Do you want to start a non-profit, or your own business? Do you want to travel and explore, or live comfortably at home? Do you want to have kids, or if you have kids, are more potentially part of your future?

_____

_____

_____

_____

At what age do you want to retire? How long do you want to be in a career before doing something else?

_____

_____

_____

_____

You are worthy of the future you want for yourself. I am not going to sugarcoat this and tell you that climbing the mountain is easy, because it isn't. It is a climb full of temptation, challenges, frustrations, and at times, failings. You are worthy of having a better future and a better life. Your family is worthy of having a better future with more opportunities. But no one is going to climb the mountain for you. You have to decide that who you want to be and what you want to do are more valuable than the immediate gratification of the things you could spend your money on instead. If you are starting to hesitate when you pull your phone out or your credit card out or your wallet out, you are making progress.

"Progress is impossible without change, and those who cannot change their minds cannot change anything."

George Bernard Shaw

What if Today is Your Unlucky Day?

You are on the road heading to work, listening to your favorite jam, when all of a sudden someone swipes across the road and hits you as you're driving. You are fine, but your car is totally wrecked, and it will be weeks before your car will be fixed. In the meanwhile, you are going to need to get around, and your insurance doesn't cover rental cars. It will be months before you get a check from the other driver, so the question is, do you have the money to cover a rental for a few weeks?

Or if perhaps today is a hot, sunny summer day, with temperatures approaching triple digits, and without warning the air conditioning just stops working. Do you have the money to repair the AC today?

Or if you get a flat tire?

Or if the heater at home quit working?

Or if some pests have decided to make your home their home?

Or imagine yourself getting really sick, and not being able to go into work until you get better. Do you have the money to go see the doctor? What if you don't, and instead of the illness taking three days to recover from, it takes three weeks because the infection spreads far beyond what it would have had you received medication. Could you afford to miss that much work? Would you have a job if you did miss that much? Or would you go in and suffer, possibly infecting your fellow team members at work with the nasty illness you contracted? Is that the "right" thing to do?

If a direct deposit didn't go through as scheduled due to a bank error, would your checks bounce? How much in finance charges from missed payments would you owe? Would those finance charges keep you from getting back on schedule?

Have you ever been in this position? Are you in it now?

Now consider this: what would it feel like if you went to bed knowing that if the car broke down, the house needed repairs, if you got sick or if there was a bank issue, you had the money to cover the expense without having to use a credit card, and without worrying whether you really had the money to pay for it? I am not saying that writing that check will be enjoyable - it never is - but I will say that being able to write that check, without reservation, is a really awesome and liberating place to be.

When you reap a healthy spending decision, you are sowing a healthy spending habit. When you reap healthy spending habits, you sow a healthy foundation to build wealth. And when you reap a healthy foundation to build wealth, you live with the peace of mind that no matter what happens, you have the resources you need when you need them. That makes it so much easier to sleep well at night.

The Best Savers in the World

Going back to the 1960's and 1970's our country used to be some of the best savers in the world. According to the U.S. Bureau of Economic Analysis, an average household would save 12-17% of what it made every year. This led to a generation that in general had strong savings and was actually prepared for retirement. As time went on, our lives became more commercialized. In the early 1980's, a television program called "Headline News" came on - the first 24/7 news company, where you could watch the news (and advertisements) anytime, day or night. Shortly after, a new station called MTV hit the airwaves, a channel dedicated to the celebration and promotion of music. This wasn't just a product placement - this was an entire station devoted to a single product medium. With the adoption of Internet in homes, we then received a whole new wave of advertising through our computers. And when we thought advertising hit saturation, no one saw just how interactive promotion could be until we invited it into our pocket. On June 29th, 2007, the first iPhone was released. Alongside notifications about our friends and family are alerts for a 40% off sale at our favorite store. We can buy anything on Amazon with just a tap or two of our phone. From ordering food to buying a new car to getting a home loan, nearly everything in our lives is at our fingertips.

It's no wonder that the 12-17% we used to save has slipped. The question is, how far have we slipped? By the 1980's, we were saving 10%, and by 2006, as we neared the credit crisis, the average American family saved just 3.2% of what it earned. That means on $10,000 earned, there would be just $320 remaining of it at the end. Even now, a decade later, according to the Organization for Economic Cooperation and Development (OECD) we only save 5.2% of what we earn, versus over 9% in Germany and 17% in Switzerland. Americans are both the biggest spenders and some of the worst savers on the planet, and make no mistake, it will cost us dearly in the long run if we do not make a major course correction.

That said, let's talk about how much you save. Giving your best estimate (and look it up if you need to) fill in the answer to the following statements.

I save _____ a month for retirement.

I save _____ a month in my checking/savings account.

I think I save:
_____ Too little
_____ About the right amount
_____ Too much for my long-term goals.

I want to save:
_____ Less money
_____ The same amount of money
_____ More money to reach my goals.

You might be saying to yourself "you only live once, so why not live it up?" The problem with that is you don't know exactly how long you will live. For many people how long they think they will live and how they think they will manage their retirement does not match up with reality. For example, a survey of people aged 65 and older conducted by AARP showed that 40% of them plan to "work until they drop." Yet in 2015, the Employee Benefit Research Institute (EBRI) found that of retirees that year, 50% of them retired early, with 82% retiring due to their own health reasons (60%) or the health of a family member/friend (22%). All the while, only 31% of retirees felt confident that they could actually afford to retire. Today, modern medicine continues to improve and the median life expectancy is steadily increasing. Failing to plan ahead could mean a lifespan of 30 or more years of financial dependence on government programs and burdening family members.

The Beginning of Something Great

You have been working so hard to identify different areas in your life that you can spend smarter, and by now you may be getting into a rhythm with the changes you are making to your daily habits. You are now ready for the next step in developing a healthy financial foundation. It is time to start building your emergency fund!

Let's start by identifying what your emergency fund is not. Your emergency fund:

- Is **NOT** a slush fund for when you feel you want something
- Is **NOT** for you to be able to charge more on your credit cards
- Is **NOT** something you touch **EXCEPT** in the event of a life emergency (not to be confused with a fashion emergency or a beer run)

Your emergency fund is an amount of money that you have saved and do not need for anything - not for your rent, and not for other bills or expenses. It is extra, and it is available to cover any unforeseen events that need, and I am emphasizing the word **NEED** to be addressed.

The purpose of this fund is twofold -
1. To force you to make a conscious decision and "break the glass" that it is in fact an emergency, and
2. To avoid the use of unnecessary lines of credit. I know credit cards are convenient to use - use the debit card instead.

When you do need to dip into the emergency fund, refill it to the full amount as soon as possible so you have that "safety net" for when something else goes wrong.

At this point, you may feel like I am advising you to live scared, which is not the case. I am advocating for you to live PREPARED and act accordingly so you do not live scared. Right now you may be on a financial tightrope that you cannot afford to lose your balance on. You may be weighed with heavy spending, little cash, and possibly a lot of debt, causing you to waste money in the form of interest payments every single month. And if you think any one of the events I described earlier is bad enough, what if two bad things were to happen right after each other? Well, if you know a storm is coming and that your power will probably be knocked out, wouldn't you buy bottled water and enough food to last a week or two? You need to do the same thing with your finances. Good things may happen to you, and bad things may happen to you too. You owe it to yourself and your family and friends to be prepared for what life may bring.

How much is in your checking/savings account? $_____

Do you currently have immediate access to at least $1,500 that is not invested in something, on a credit card, or already assigned to pay another expense? Yes / No (circle one)

If you circled no, commit to a date where you will have your emergency fund built. Be realistic about your time line. Write that date in the following statement, and put that date on a sticky note for your mirror, refrigerator, computer screen - anywhere you can see it and be reminded of it. This is now a financial top priority, because not having one can be costly.

I do not have an emergency fund yet, but I will have $1,500 in an emergency fund saved no later than _____. I will save every penny possible to reach this goal as quickly as possible.

This money is something that you will already own (not borrow) and could tap into in the event of an emergency. Rebuilding your financial foundation needs to be your top priority now that you are starting to save more money. Start by building your emergency fund to $1,500. Why $1,500? Because $1,500 can cover the cost of many major emergencies, and maybe even multiple emergencies if necessary. Eventually, strong emergency savings will consist of 3-6 months of expenses, but $1,500 is a good starting point for building the fund.

Almost half of Americans don't have an emergency fund at all, so it is up to you to break that trend. You cannot predict the future, but we are certain that our future is uncertain. Being prepared starts by starting to build your financial savings, and the first step to do that is to build an emergency fund.

Ask and Ye May Receive
(a better rate)

Have you ever wondered why the value of your car goes down over time, but the insurance cost for your car stays the same? Or why a cable company can afford to give you a promotional rate on service for two years, but then charges you up to 100% more for the same service the day after the promotion ends?

Many service providers rely on the idea that there is a natural tendency for customers to NOT ask for a better price or a better deal. In America, asking for a better rate or negotiating the cost of a service is not a natural part of doing business for most consumers. In many businesses and in other parts of the world, negotiating is not only widely accepted but in many cases is a normal, even expected part of shopping.

What's even more interesting is that you are willing to negotiate under certain conditions, but not others. You do not regularly check for a better insurance rate, but will haggle the price of the car you want to buy (and insure) at the car dealership. You do not ask for a better price on your Internet or mobile service, yet you bid on items on eBay, and use Priceline to "Name Your Own Price" on a hotel room for a vacation, and use Amazon to buy items at a lower price and to price match when shopping at a competitor. It's not that you cannot or do not negotiate; you have just created invisible barriers for yourself based on when you think it is appropriate to negotiate.

NEW THINKING: IT IS ALWAYS APPROPRIATE TO NEGOTIATE!

It is not disrespectful to ask for the best deal possible. It is respectful to your bank account. It is being a good steward of your resources to get the most value possible for what you spend. This does not give you a license to spend, on the perception that you "saved so much," or what I like to call the "Kohl's Effect" where the retailer thrives on what the customer perceives are major discounts they have found. It does give you a license once you have narrowed down what you are spending money on to get the most out of the money you are spending and save more money if possible.

During the next two days, go through this list and call the provider of whatever services apply to you. If the company offers to complete a survey after the call, say yes. When you get a customer service representative on the phone, say the following:

"My name is [your name] and I am a loyal customer of [insert company name]. I really hope you can help me today, because I have a problem. I believe I am paying too much for my service, and would like the best price you can offer me for my account."

Notice that I did not say "get angry" or "threaten to leave" or "throw a temper tantrum." In fact, this approach is exactly the OPPOSITE of that. You are engaging that service representative to help you solve a problem, which makes them a partner working with you, not an opponent to attempt to defeat. By approaching this in a non-adversarial way you are disarming the customer service representative from using any sort of defensive tactics and encouraging them to think about ways they can actually help you. Moreover, you are rare in that you are actually being nice, calm, rational, and pleasant to talk with, meaning that they will not only want to talk to you longer, but are incentivized by the respect you are showing them to make sure you leave the line feeling helped. Lastly, you are that customer service member's best hope for positive ratings, which may mean incentives and job security for being so helpful to you.

WARNING: Many times, a service provider will try to add or "bun-dle" services as a means of offering you a "savings." This is another common sales tactic that, unless it actually does save you money, you should politely refuse. The goal is not to buy more things - the goal is to reduce your bill at the end of each month/year.

Today and tomorrow, reach out to the following service providers and ask for their best price. After each call, write down how much money you saved a month from that call, and total the amount of money you saved from all of your calls at the end of the list.

Day 17 - The First 3 Calls for Better Rates

Here is the script to assist you - use it!

"My name is [your name] and I am a loyal customer of [insert company name]. I really hope you can help me today, because I have a problem. I believe I am paying too much for my service, and would like the best price you can offer me for my account."

1. Cable/Internet provider. $_____/month saved!

2. Phone service provider. $_____/month saved!

3. Insurance provider(s). $_____/month saved!

Day 18 - The Last 3 Calls for Better Rates

4. Gym membership provider. $_____/month saved!

5. Apartment rent/monthly fees. $_____/month saved!

6. Medical and Legal bills. $_____/month saved!

Total Amount Saved: $_____/month saved!

A Plan for Presents and Promotions

There is no feeling quite like getting a windfall. It could be a financial gift from a relative to celebrate a special milestone in your life, earning a bonus for a job well done, or earning a promotion that carries with it an increase in pay. It is one thing to have people tell you they appreciate the work you do; it feels even better when that translates into you having more money.

It is so tempting when you earn a bonus or receive a gift to treat it as "extra" and that "you can do whatever you want with it." And to an extent, it's true, you CAN indeed do anything you want with it. But should you? I think by the time you have gotten to this point in the book, you probably know what that answer is. But even knowing that you should not go on a massive shopping spree or run out and buy a new car immediately still does not tell you what to do with the funds Here is a list of a few big ways you could put your money to better use.

1. Build your emergency fund. If you do not have 3-6 months worth of expenses in an emergency fund, consider saving the money for a rainy day. We never know when something good or bad can happen, but we can plan for the certainty of uncertainty by having a reasonable amount of money ready if something bad happens.

2. Pay off debt! If you have debt, especially if it's credit card debt or school debt, using the money to pay that down means paying less interest and becoming debt-free much more quickly.

3. Max out contributions to your retirement funds. Maybe you have saved some money but haven't quite reached your annual goals for retirement saving. Not only will your future self be thankful for saving today, but you may receive a tax deduction as well.

In the space below, write a one-sentence statement that says exactly what you are going to do if you receive an unexpected financial bonus.

"When I receive a financial gift or bonus, I will ...

_____

_____

_____

Two Roads to Earning More

Every person reading this book has a unique set of needs and priorities. I understand completely that you probably don't want to take on another job, at least not permanently. However, if you are in credit card debt, realize that right now you are paying on average 16.1% annually on whatever debt you are carrying. That means that for every $1,000 in credit card debt you have, you may be paying $161 per year ($13.41 per month) for every $1,000 you owe to pay the interest on that debt - not pay the debt off, just the interest. According to the U.S. Census Bureau and the Federal Reserve, the average credit card debt per household in America is $16,000. According to NerdWallet, this means that on average American households pay over $1,300 a year in credit card interest charges. That is a whole lot of money to pay for a whole lot of nothing!

You may be thinking at this point, "Steven, your book is about spending smarter, so why are you telling me to get another job? That isn't spending!" You are right, getting a job is not directly about spending money. But let's think about this - if you have credit card debt, you are passively spending that credit card interest every single month when your credit card company charges you. By taking on a part-time job to pay down this debt, or to earn more to fund your savings, you are making the effort to have more resources to reduce spending on interest charges that get you nothing. You are now building your financial foundation quicker to reduce debt so you can move on to something bigger financially such as saving and investing. That sounds like pretty smart spending to me!

There are two ways to help you earn more.

1. Decrease expenses. You have started to do this and will continue to do so by spending smarter.

2. Increase revenue. Take on more work to earn more pay to get where you want to be financially more quickly.

Think back to your priorities, what you listed were the most important things in your life. Taking on some extra work to push through the things that will hold you back the most. The longer you let them fester is a good thing. A part-time job does not have to be an overly taxing job either. Perhaps that's mowing lawns, painting apartments, delivering pizzas, or working some hours during the holidays at a retail store (many times, seasonal hours will pay time and a half or double time and will provide food, making it even more lucrative). Just be careful that whatever it is you decide to do is a real job. You do not need to become a traveling salesperson for kitchen gadgets or makeup, where you will more than likely be asked to take on inventory or a loan to begin; this is a trap, so avoid it.

Part-Time Sweat For Long-Term Potential Benefits

Whether you are in credit card debt or not, but especially if you are, write down three part-time jobs you will pursue as a means of increasing income. Think 8-10 hours of total extra work a week - that's an extra $4,000 a year that you can be building an emergency fund, paying down credit card debt, and getting your financial house back in order as quickly as you can.

Part time job #1: _____

Part time job #2: _____

Part time job #3: _____

I will earn $_____ more every month because I was willing to put some sweat equity now into building toward my future financial goals.

Right now, you may be on a financial tightrope. If you fall, it could be absolutely devastating. The quicker we can get you off the tightrope and safely onto solid ground, the better. It takes a different approach to life to expect a different result. My challenge to you with this topic is to get aggressive with earning and smarter with spending so you can be one of the best savers in the world.

Debt the Destroyer

I believe one of the greatest threats to your financial well-being is debt. Debt saps away from what you earn. When you go into debt, you are trading hours of your life, hours of what you earn through the labor you toil with every day, for the right to acquire something now with the promise of repayment later.

The problem is, pretty much everything we acquire with debt loses value over time. From cars and furniture to home theater equipment, technology, appliances - none of these things gain value as you use them But the salespeople are so good at convincing you that you need these items. When you go into a store a sale will indeed take place - either the salesperson will convince you to buy the item or you will convince them that you will not buy the item. The next section will guide you on how to avoid purchases you do not actually need to make because you will know the tactics salespeople use to try and persuade you.

REMEMBER: Either you will sell the salesperson on not buying the item, or the salesperson will sell you on buying it. Who do you want to win?

Sales Tactics 101

When you go to a car dealership or a furniture store, what do you think of? What does that experience remind you of? Take a minute to close your eyes and think about the people you interacted with and how they made you feel as you looked at things and as you considered making a purchase.

Did you get tense or nervous inside, like you might be walking into a trap? Did you think about how the prices were more than you wanted to pay, but the salesperson would check with the manager to see what they could do for you? And when you got done shopping, did you feel like you made a good purchase, or did you wonder whether or not you actually got a good deal at all?

I am going to guess that yes, you were nervous about walking into a trap and that you probably did not feel like you made a good purchase when you walked out. And to be blunt, someone making you feel this way really sucks. Many businesses use talking points and tactics to sell a product or service instead of simply serving their customers.. They ask leading questions to try and trap you into their line of thinking about an item, and then use their talking points to make you feel inferior by not taking their offer, when their "deal" may indeed be a very bad bargain for you.

Today, you are going to learn many of the tactics salespeople use so that you are prepared to handle what may come your way. These are some of the most common phrases and ideas used to convince customers to purchase products and services. They validate a desire, create a false sense of need, or try to break the numbers down in a way that makes the cost more reasonable than it actually is. Today, I want you to read this list aloud five times today. The first two times, read this list to yourself. The next two times, read it to a family member or a friend (and more people if you want). The final time, before you go to bed, write a short response that tells how you will respond when someone uses this line or tactic on you.

1. "You will get so much use out of it."

You will probably get just as much out of a used model or the model you already have.

Your response: _____

_____

_____

2. "You won't have to worry about it breaking down."

While you may not pay for repairs immediately on a new car, you still have costs involved in owning any transportation. Vehicles need tires, brakes, oil changes, fuel - all of these things cost money. And according to edmunds.com, the moment your new car leaves the lot it depreciates on average 11% of it's value. On a $25,000 vehicle, that's $2,750 - way more than it would cost to cover the vast majority of major repairs, not to mention a number of small repairs if your fortune turns sour.

Your response: _____

_____

_____

3. "It only costs $X a year or pennies a day."

That doesn't change the price. Hitting the division symbol on a calculator does not make a major purchase any more or less affordable

Your response:

_____

_____

4. "With a 0% interest rate, you can afford this. It doesn't cost you more."

Within 2 years of you driving the new car off the lot, the car may have lost 40% of the price you paid for it. That is not zero cost! The interest rate just gauges how much MORE you are going to pay for that item depending on how long it takes you to pay it off. It does not make the item more affordable and it does not account for the depreciation of the item over time. And if you lose your job or something unfortunate happens and you are unable to earn an income, that loan can go from being "affordable" to becoming very unaffordable in a hurry!

Your response:

_____

Keep reviewing and practicing your responses so that they become built up like a defensive reflex. The best way to avoid these types of purchases is simply to not go into stores that put you in these types of situations. However, when you are in a high-pressure sales environment, you are now armed with the confidence to identify when you are being "sold" something. Make a choice that aligns with your goals, not the salesperson's.

You Must Face Your Fears

"One of the greatest discoveries a man makes, one of his great surprises, is to find he can do what he was afraid he couldn't do."
- Henry Ford

"You are only afraid if you are not in harmony with yourself. People are afraid because they have never owned up to themselves."
- Hermann Hesse

While major purchases are a big culprit for acquiring debt, common day-to-day expenses create a monster all their own. We have been trained that it is so much easier to go out to eat to pacify ourselves and simplify our lives than make a once a week grocery run. We are creatures of habit, bombarded by ideas for new habits with advertisements literally embedded in how we communicate (our phones, on the Internet, in our email). You have broken that spending down and you became more aware of the pitfall. This is your reminder to keep shopping for groceries, and to not trade back your money and financial well-being for food that you can make at home yourself.

So that all said, when was the last time you looked at your credit card bills? I am not just talking about the balance, but actually read your credit card statement, line by line?

Does that idea terrify you? You and most people.

There is one clear reason why. It's because you did it. You swiped the card, and you spent the money, and there's no one else to own it but you. But it's time to face that fear. It's time to look that fear in the eye and realize that this monster will not go away on its own, realize that you cannot fight what you do not know, and you need to look and look carefully if you want to know what you need to know to slay this beast. There is no one else to fight this fight. You have to fight this fight, and if you intend on building a strong financial foundation, you have no choice BUT to win this fight.

Write a paragraph, completing each of the following statements.

I do/do not (circle one) fear looking at my credit card bill because ...

_____

_____

_____

_____

_____

_____

_____

If I do not look at my credit card bill, what will happen to me?

_____

_____

_____

_____

_____

_____

_____

I will look at my credit card bill on _____ **date.**

(Put tomorrow's date)

You are a smarter spender, and this is another step toward you becoming financially independent and in a position to build real wealth. You have come so far already, and yet the journey ahead may feel so long. And that's okay. But continuing to live with this burden, continuing to allow high-interest debt to eat into what you earn, that is not okay, and I know you want a better life and a better future for yourself. You will do it - you need to believe in you because I believe in you. I may not have met you, but I know that if you have gotten to this point in this book, and have done everything asked of you up to this point, you have already shown that you are exceptional and different than how most people live. That is where the trust I have in you comes from.

The Weekly Credit Card Checklist

Credit cards are a difficult beast to slay. On Day 7, I discussed the idea that mobile applications and credit cards are difficult to manage because you cannot "see" your money being spent when you pay with one of these devices. I recommended taking at least your weekly food budget and using cash to pay for those expenses. I also suggested using separate cash wallets for each discretionary expense category, while setting mandatory expenses like your rent or mortgage on automatic payment each month.

Credit card statements are also hard to see, but for an entirely different reason. Credit card statements are hard to see because you do not want to see them. Credit card statements are painful to see, because you know that you spend too much. You know that the content of a credit card statement includes all of your spending sins. And yet, you hope that by ignoring what the bill says, ignoring what is on the statement, that eventually it will just fix itself and go away.

However, these last three weeks have brought tremendous changes in your spending behaviors. You have made substantial and thoughtful changes to decrease your spending. With each passing day, you are becoming more aware of how your day-to-day decisions impact your finances long-term. You know that the future you want is at stake. You are making smarter spending choices today that sow smarter spending habits for tomorrow that reap your financial future.

You are now ready to open the credit card statement.

As you open your credit card statement and start looking at your spending, here are four habits I suggest you start doing. These habits are more than just a to-do list; they are a weapon, a sword tempered and sharpened to cut through crappy spending. Once a week, spend fifteen minutes to complete these three actions (repeat this process for each card you have).

1. Look at your statement. Once a week (pick a day and time to do this) spend fifteen minutes going over your weekly expenses. Practically every card allows you to see purchases instantly online, so read, line by line, what you charged to your card this week. By doing this line by line review, you are starting to put a name to every dollar you spend. When you go out, and you see the name of a business, you'll begin to associate it with the cost it generates on your potential savings. That's a good thing.

2. Identify any credit card fraud. If you see a charge you don't recognize, investigate it! If you cannot track down that company, call your credit card company and report the unauthorized expense.

3. Highlight your expenses. A way to "see" good and bad expenses is to use a green highlighter for good expenses and an orange highlighter for bad expenses. Rent, electric, reasonable groceries, fuel for your vehicle all get green highlights. Weekly clothing shopping trips, Starbucks runs and more blu-ray discs get the orange highlighter. Work to reduce the number of orange lines each week.

You deserve to be free of this debt. You deserve to be able to cut this burden from your life, to regain control of your resources and owe no one a portion of your hard-earned dollars from the hours you work of your life. But at the end of the day, no one but you created the problem, and no one but you can buckle down, look that fear in the eye, learn what you're doing, address it, and spend smarter today so that you can be living better tomorrow.

You Are the Hero!

"Only when we are no longer afraid do we begin to live."
Dorothy Thompson

"Heroes need monsters to establish their heroic credentials. You need something scary to overcome."
- Margaret Atwood

Today, you are going to do something truly heroic. You probably didn't wake up thinking about how heroic you are going to be today, but you are.

Do you want to know how I know that?

I know that because today is more than just another day; it is a test. It is a test of will, of your personal fortitude and strength, your ability to take a gigantic leap, a titanic stride that only a true hero can make. Are you ready for the monster unknown? Prepare yourself - here we go!

In order to conquer your debts and conquer your spending, you have to know what they are for real. Yesterday, you categorized your statements based on what you are spending. As you spend less on things you don't need, it's time to use the money saved from cutting costs to pay off the debts that are keeping you from eventually being able to invest and build toward the lifestyle you want.

Today, we are not looking to slay every monster. No no, we are hunting a specific one - the plastic monster. They may be shiny, and have fancy pictures on them, or they may say words like "Executive" or "Platinum" to try to make you feel important, even though you already are important and that their pandering to your ego is just another sales tactic. They helped facilitate this mess, but it was you who is truly responsible because you swiped the card or pushed "Add to Cart" on your mobile device.

And now it's time to start on the path to defeat them, once and for all.

Your Credit Card Monster Inventory

In the lines below, write down all the credit cards you have. I also want you to use your credit card statement to write down the interest rate of the card and the balance remaining on that card.

Name of Card	Interest Rate	Balance

Day 24

Name of Card	Interest Rate	Balance

Which Monster Do You Slay First?

On the 23rd day, the credit card statement was broken down.
On the 24th day, the list of credit monsters was made.
And on the 25th day, you will arrange the monsters for the slaughter!

Using the list of all the credit monsters from yesterday, rewrite the list in order of largest balance to smallest balance. You might be asking yourself "why did he make me write the interest rate yesterday?" I wanted you to see just how generous you have been to these companies. I am sure they are very appreciative, but it's time to no longer be their servant.

Name of Card	Balance

Name of Card	Balance

Starting with the bottom of the list, that's where you are going to start paying debt off. Pay the minimums on the rest of the cards, but start by paying the smallest card/balance first. As you finish one card, that's only going to increase how quickly you can pay off the second card, and so on. Your payments should increase over timen until there aren't any more payments to make. At that point, you are no longer a servant to these companies.

DAY 26

We All Need Somebody to Lean On (so make sure they are strong!)

Over the past few weeks, you have taken some very aggressive actions toward spending smarter that may have translated into some significant changes in how you live your life. In fact, for most readers I expect that several of these changes are a drastic departure from what was happening a few weeks ago. Yet on average, it takes people 66 days to adopt a new habit, meaning that even after you finish this book, it will take another couple of months for these habits to set in. That's a lot of opportunity to slip back into old routines, so you need to defend against that threat.

One way to do that is to go through this book a second time after you finish it in a few days. That's a good start, but I am a huge fan of having people to cheer you on, people you can rely on to support you and to talk to when there is pressure and it gets tough to stay disciplined (and trust me, if you have not felt it already it will happen at some point). Identify a Smarter Spending accountability partner by looking for someone you can confide in and trust to talk about your day-to-day challenges with spending smarter.

You need to be careful about who you pick for this role. If you surround yourself with someone who is irresponsible, don't be surprised if they try to pull you into their problems, their issues, and add nothing to your life, not support you improving yourself, or worse yet - attempt to sabotage your efforts by becoming jealous and acting negatively toward you because you are trying to make your life better. If you partner with someone who is financially responsible, what do you think will happen with your finances? And what do you think will happen to your financial decision making if the person you lean on is financially irresponsible?

Imagine dressing up in your finest clothes with perfume or cologne, and then you walk into a garbage dump. You may not touch any of the garbage, but if you stand in the dump for a couple hours and then walk out, you're probably going to stink. This happens when it comes to the people we surround ourselves with to. Will you still smell nice or will you stink after you are influenced by your accountability partner? Don't be stinky!

My financial accountability partner will be _____

and I will ask them on _____ **to be my Smarter Spending**

accountability partner. *(today's date)*

Is this person a superstar? If not, why did you pick someone that is not a superstar? Are you scared to have a superstar on your team? Many people are - it can bruise your ego a bit to be around someone is wealthier, smarter, more successful than you are right now.

But here's the catch - by being around that person more, you can learn from them how they got to where they are at. The fascinating thing is that for many successful people, what they do to be successful is not terribly complicated, and they happily share what they do with other people. As my friend and successful small-business owner Steve Port said to me, "I don't want a bigger piece of the pie; instead, I want to make more pie. That way, by default my piece is bigger."

Now go call that trusted person and make them your Smarter Spending Accountability Partner!

Less Spending
= More Ammunition

You have spent a considerable amount of time learning how to curb spending. You have progressed through a mile-deep approach into areas consumers spend the most money on - food costs, services, conveniences and financing fees (credit card interest/late fees). As intense as this process probably felt, I will venture to guess that you made major inroads that helped you shed spending, giving you more room to build an emergency fund and start paying off your credit card debt. And I bet that feels pretty good.

Well, I don't know about you, but I am not satisfied with pretty good. Going from a D or an F to a B+ is certainly an accomplishment, but I know you can do even more. I know you can be head of the class and earn that A. In order to earn the A, you will need to be aware of everything you spend; and take the same approach, the same level of scrutiny, to other areas of your life.

In today's activity, figure out how much you make and how much you spend in specific categories each month. I want you to then go category by category and try to find ways to improve the amount you spend each month.

Income
Salary, wages, tips _____
Child support _____
Other income _____
Total Monthly Income _____

Expenses
Mortgage or rent _____
Utilities *(gas, water, electric)* _____
Phone/Internet _____
Child Care/Education _____
Car Payment _____
Car Maintenance _____
Fuel _____
Food _____
Clothing _____
Furnishings _____
Personal Care _____
Health Care _____
Debt Payments _____
Entertainment _____
Charity/Gifts _____
Other Expenses _____
Total Expenses _____

Your Net Income

_____ - _____ = _____

Total Income *Total Expenses* *Ammunition*

Write down one more thing you are willing to cut back on to save more money.

_____

_____

How much money/month will you save from this final trade-off?

$_____

I also challenge you, especially if you have credit card debt, to take on a one-day or two-day a week part time job to help you pay that debt off faster. It's time to get truly mean, lean, and aggressive, because it's your future on the line.

SCOREBOARD!

"If it doesn't matter who wins or loses, then why do they keep score?"
- Vince Lombardi

"I've missed more than 9,000 shots in my career. I've lost almost 300 games. 26 times, I have been trusted to take the game winning shot and missed. I have failed over and over and over again in my life. And that is why I succeed."
- Michael Jordan

It is now time to see just how well you have done over the past four weeks, but the only way you can actually see whether you won or lost starts by keeping score. You have been keeping score the whole time we have been together, but focused on daily activities. Today, it is time to see just how much money you are saving every single month through the new spending and earning habits you have acquired. For each of the following habits, go back to the day listed and at the end of that day, you should have written a number for how much money you saved each month by changing your behavior. Take the numbers from each section and write them down on the appropriate line, and then add up the total amount saved at the end of the list.

Day 3: Eating Smarter to Spend Smarter	$_____
Day 4: Is Starbucks Sipping Away Your Savings?	$_____
Day 5: Make Lunch Boxes Great Again	$_____
Day 6: Date Night Does Not Mean Debt Night	$_____
Day 12: Trading Back Convenience for Cost	$_____
Day 13: Subscription Services Suck!	$_____
Day 14: Conserve Energy and Save Green	$_____
Day 17-18: Ask and Ye May Receive (a better rate)	$_____
Day 20: Part-Time Sweat For Long-Term Benefits	$_____
Day 27: Less Spending = More Ammunition	$_____
Total Money Saved Monthly by Spending Smarter	$_____

_____ **X 12 =** _____

Total Saved   *12 Months*   **TOTAL SAVED**
THIS YEAR BY
SPENDING SMARTER!

Look at this! Look at what you have done over the past four weeks! You should be so proud and pleased with the changes you have made, changes in your day-to-day life, changes in how you live and how you think about the money you make. And as you stick to these new behaviors month after month, you will save more for the goals that actually matter to you. Let's review together what you value, the reasons behind why you have chosen to make these changes in your habits and in your lifestyle.

What are the three things that are most important to you? (Day 12)

1. _____

2. _____

3. _____

How do you think you might want to live as you get older? What sort of house or apartment do you want to live in? Any particular vehicle you want to drive, or clothes you want to wear, or a part of the country you want to be in? Small town, big city, in the mountains, or on a beach?

_____

_____

_____

_____

_____

_____

_____

_____

_____

What do you want to do? What level of lifestyle you want? What types of things might you want to do? Do you want to start a non-profit organization, or launch your own business? Do you want to travel and explore, or live comfortably at home? Do you want to have kids, or if you have kids, are more potentially part of your future?

_____

_____

_____

_____

_____

_____

_____

_____

At what age do you want to retire? How long do you want to be in a career before doing something different?

_____

_____

_____

_____

_____

_____

_____

_____

CONCLUSION

The Journey Has Just Begun

Two roads diverged in a yellow wood,
And sorry I could not travel both
And be one traveler, long I stood
And looked down one as far as I could
To where it bent in the undergrowth;

Then took the other, as just as fair,
And having perhaps the better claim,
Because it was grassy and wanted wear;
Though as for that the passing there
Had worn them really about the same,

And both that morning equally lay
In leaves no step had trodden black.
Oh, I kept the first for another day!
Yet knowing how way leads on to way,
I doubted if I should ever come back.

Conclusion

I shall be telling this with a sigh
Somewhere ages and ages hence:
Two roads diverged in a wood, and I—
I took the one less traveled by,
And that has made all the difference.

- The Road Not Taken by Robert Frost

So here we are, the end of the road. We walked a path together, a path that many Americans do not have the knowledge, or the courage, to take. Many Americans spend nearly every dollar they earn and save very little money at all. Many Americans have nearly their entire lives leveraged by debt, and live paycheck to paycheck, or very close to that line.

But you are special. You are not like many Americans.

You have tackled what you eat, striving to consume less. You have tackled your credit cards, attacking them, and paying them off. You have dissected your family budget, trimming expenses each step, and you may have even taken an additional job to elevate your earnings to build the emergency fund and pay that debt off all the quicker. Within months, or maybe a year or so if you have quite a bit of debt, you will get to the point where that credit card debt is done, where the monsters are finally gone once and for all.

And then what? Is this the end of our journey?

No, this is only the beginning. This gets you to a point where you switch from digging out of a hole to starting to build up your net worth. Here is a list of the next steps in store for you.

Steven Briggs

Prior to opening his financial practice, Steven was a teacher and educational administrator for eight years, where he advised public schools and individual families about college preparedness. Steven volunteers for the National Multiple Sclerosis Society, Extra Life - a charity benefiting the Children's Miracle Network, and as a middle-school MATHCOUNTS team coach.

$ 99

ACKNOWLEDGEMENTS

To Amber, my love, for your incredible love and support throughout this process and for putting up with my "inner child."

To Megan Robinson, who has shown incredible patience in working with me to transform thoughts and ideas into this prudent guide.

To Chaffee-Thanh Nguyen and Brian T. Wolf, who started me on the path to writing a book in the first place.

To the millions and millions of people who struggle with their finances, but have the courage and work ethic and guts to work harder and live smarter to build a better future for themselves and those who come after them.

To my family and friends, who have shown continuous love and support throughout the process of opening my practice, and now writing this first book.

You are my rock, my pillar I have always been able to count on, and this work would not have happened without you.

Thank you.